The Library of SPIDERS™

The Crab Spider

Alice B. McGinty

The Rosen Publishing Group's
PowerKids Press™
New York

To Zachary

Published in 2002 by The Rosen Publishing Group, Inc.
29 East 21st Street, New York, NY 10010

First Edition

Book Design: Emily Muschinske
Project Consultant: Kathleen Reid Zeiders
Project Editor: Emily Raabe

Photo Credits: Cover, title page, pp. 6 (bottom), 9 (bottom) © Scott Smith/Animals Animals; p. 5 (crab) © Corbis; pp 5 (top left, inset right and lower right), 6 (top right and top left), 10 (lower left), 11© David Liebman; p. 7 © W. Cheng/Animals Animals; p. 9 (left) © John Gerlach/Animals Animals; p. 9 (top right) © John Specker/Animals Animals; p. 10 (top left) © Richard Kolar/Animals Animals; p. 10 (center) © Robert Noonan; pp. 10 (lower right), 13 (left), 14 (right), 15 , 21 (top left and bottom) © A. B. Sheldon; p. 13 (upper right) © Leen Van Der Slik/Animals Animals; p. 13 (lower right) © J. A. L Cooke/Animals Animals; pp. 14 (left), 17 (top left) © E. R. Degginger/Animals Animals; p. 17 (lower right) © Bill Beatty/Animals Animals; p. 17 (lower left and top right) © Hans Pfletschinger/Peter Arnold; p. 18 © Patty Murray/Animals Animals; p, 21 (left) © Ted Levin/ Animals Animals.

McGinty, Alice B.
    The crab spider / Alice B. McGinty.— 1st ed.
        p. cm. — (The library of spiders)
    ISBN 0-8239-5570-2 (lib. bdg.)
    1. Crab spiders—Juvenile literature. [1. Crab spiders. 2. Spiders.]
I. Title
    QL458.4 .M43 2002
    595.4′4—dc21

                                            00-011694

Manufactured in the United States of America

Contents

The Crab Spider

It is not hard to figure out how crab spiders got their name. They look like crabs! Crab spiders can move like crabs too. They shuffle backwards and from side to side, just like real crabs.

Giant crab spiders can be over three inches (7.7cm) long with their legs spread out. Most crab spiders are tiny, though. They can hide inside the center of a flower.

Crab spiders live all over the world. Most of them, especially giant crab spiders, live in warm, **tropical** places. Still there are about 225 kinds of crab spiders in North America, including 12 kinds of giant crab spiders.

crab

crab spider

(Top left) This white crab spider is hiding in a white flower.

(Right) Crab spiders often hold their first two sets of legs away from their bodies.

(Top right and below) These crab spiders show up clearly against this green leaf and orange flower.

(Above) Can you see the yellow crab spider in this picture? Its yellow color helps it to blend in with this yellow flower.

Evolving Spiders

Spiders appeared on earth about 395 million years ago! Over the years, spiders have evolved, or changed, to help them survive. Scientists believe that crab spiders **evolved** in several different ways.

Some crab spiders ran among plants to catch **prey**. They developed long bodies and long legs to help them run quickly. They grew tufts of hair on their claws to help them grip and climb well.

Other crab spiders sat on plants and waited for prey. Their bodies evolved to become short and wide. Their front legs became long and strong to grab prey. Their back legs became shorter and weaker. These short, strong crab spiders did not grow tufts of hair on their claws, because they did not need to climb things very often.

(Right) This giant crab spider lives on the Solomon Islands, near Australia, in the Pacific Ocean.

Crab spiders have very weak chelicerae. Their venom is so strong, however, that crab spiders can kill insects that are much bigger than they are.

The Crab Spider's Body

A spider's body has two main parts. The front part of the spider's body is called the **cephalothorax**. The spider's brain and stomach are in this body part. The spider also has eight legs, which are attached to the cephalothorax. The back part of the spider's body is called the **abdomen**. The spider's heart, lungs, and silk glands are in the abdomen. The spider has six **spinnerettes** on its abdomen that release silk.

Spiders have two **chelicerae**, or jaws. The chelicerae have sharp fangs on their ends. These fangs inject **venom** into the spider's prey.

Crab spiders come in many different shapes and colors.

cephalothorax

abdomen

chelicerae

The Crab Spider's Home

DID YOU KNOW?

Crab spiders are known as free-living, or wandering spiders. This means that they do not catch their food in webs. Instead, crab spiders hunt for their food.

Many crab spiders live on plants, trees, or flowers. Crab spiders do not build webs. They simply stay in places where they can catch prey. One kind of crab spider spends its time lying head down along a blade of grass. It hugs the grass with its legs and flings itself onto insects that pass by.

Some crab spiders wander around and do not have homes at all. When the spider wants to rest, it squeezes its flat body under a rock, in a crack, or beneath the bark of a tree. Some crab spiders rest at night. Others rest during the day.

These pictures show crab spiders sitting on plants, waiting for prey. Crab spiders may sit for days on the same flower without moving until an insect comes along. The insect will go to the flower looking for pollen, and will get captured by the patient crab spider.

(Right) Even this butterfly is not too large for the crab spider's powerful venom.

(Left) This crab spider has captured a bumblebee and injected it with venom.

Ambushing Prey

Some crab spiders are called **ambushing** spiders. They hide and wait for prey to come near. Then they attack their prey!

Many ambushing crab spiders hide on flowers. Usually, the spider is the same color as the flower. The spider sits very still with its front legs stretched out. When an insect lands on the flower to drink nectar, the crab spider grabs it. The spider bites the back of the insect's neck with its fangs. The spider's venom quickly **paralyzes** the insect. The venom also turns the insides of the insect to liquid. The spider hides underneath the insect while it sucks out the insect's insides.

(Right) Crab spiders will hide in a flower all day, waiting for prey to land.

Finding a Mate

Many crab spiders mate in the spring. The male crab spider finds a female crab spider. Before mating, the male spider may gently wrap the female spider in a silk web. The male crab spider is much smaller than the female crab spider. The silk web protects the male spider in case the female spider tries to eat him.

In early summer, the female crab spider spins a silk bowl and lays her eggs in the bowl. She rolls silk around the bowl until she has formed an oval sac. The female spider guards her egg sac carefully. Most female crab spiders die before their eggs hatch.

(Right) In this picture, you can see how much bigger the female crab spider is compared to the male.

16

male

female

(Top left) This large female is eating the smaller male crab spider.

(Top right) This is a female crab spider guarding her egg sac.

(Above) This male crab spider is hard for predators to see on an orange leaf.

(Above) This is a giant crab spider. She is guarding the egg sac that has her babies inside it.

Baby Crab Spiders

After the spider eggs hatch, the **spiderlings** chew a hole in the egg sac and climb out. Some baby crab spiders balloon. This means that they climb to a high spot, like the top of a flower. They release silk from their spinnerettes. The silk catches the breeze and carries the spiderlings up in the air. The spiderlings will live wherever they land.

A spider's body is covered with a hard **exoskeleton**. As each spiderling grows, its exoskeleton becomes too small. The spiderling must molt, or shed its old skin. The spiderlings will molt many times before they are fully grown.

The Crab Spider's Enemies

The crab spider's main enemies are birds and mud dauber wasps. Crab spiders use **camouflage** to protect themselves from **predators**. The spider blends in with its surroundings, so predators can not see it. For example, pink crab spiders live on pink flowers, so they look like part of the flower.

A white crab spider can even change color to camouflage itself. If it sits on a yellow flower, in about a week the spider will become yellow. If it is put back on a white flower, the spider will turn white again.

Can you see the crab spiders in these pictures? The spiders have the same colors and patterns as the flowers that they have chosen to hide out on. This makes it very hard for the crab spider's predators to see the spider.

Crab Spiders and People

The small crab spiders that live on flowers are hard to see. They are well camouflaged! Keep an eye out for a flower with insect shells underneath it, or for an insect sitting very still on a flower. Underneath that insect may be a crab spider finishing its meal.

All spiders help people by eating harmful insects. Giant crab spiders are especially helpful. Many live in houses where they hide their flat bodies behind pictures or in cracks. They come out at night and eat roaches and other bothersome insects.

While crab spiders may bite people, most bites are not known to be harmful. Some crab spider bites have caused minor reactions in people. For the most part, these interesting and colorful spiders are a great help to humans.

Glossary

abdomen (AB-duh-min) A spider's rear body part. In humans, this is the lower belly.

ambushing (AM-bush) Attacking from a hiding place.

camouflage (KA-muh-flaj) The color or pattern of an animal's fur, feathers, or skin, that allow it to blend in and not to be seen.

cephalothorax (sef-uh-low-THOR-ax) A spider's front body part made up of its head and chest.

chelicerae (kih-LIH-se-re) A spider's "jaws" containing the fangs.

evolved (ee-VOLVD) To have changed or developed over many years.

exoskeleton (ek-oh-SKEH-lah-ton) The hard outer shell of a spider's body.

paralyzes (PAR-uh-lyzez) Causes something to be unable to move.

predators (PREH-duh-terz) Animals that kill other animals for food.

prey (PRAY) An animal which is hunted by another animal for food.

spiderlings (SPY-der-lings) Baby spiders.

spinnerettes (spin-uhr-ETZ) Organs located on the rear of the spider's abdomen which release silk.

tropical (TRAH-pih-kul) An area that is very hot and humid.

venom (VEN-nom) A poison passed from one animal to another through a bite or a sting.

Index

Web Sites

For more information on crab spiders, check out these Web sites:

http://entowww.tamu.edu/extension/youth/bug/bug165.html
www.discovery.com/exp/spiders/zooms/backyardpic2.html